HELP IS ON THE WAY FOR:

Library Skills

Written by Marilyn Berry
Pictures by Bartholomew

CHILDRENS PRESS™
CHICAGO

Childrens Press
School and Library Edition

Copyright ©1985 by Marilyn Berry
Institute of Living Skills, Fallbrook, CA
All rights reserved.
Printed in the United States of America.
ISBN 0-516-03235-6

Executive Producers: Ron Berry and Joy Berry
Producer: Ellen Klarberg
Editors: Nancy Cochran and Susan Motycka
Consultants: Kathleen McBride, Maureen Dryden, and Donna Fisher
Design: Abigail Johnston
Typesetting: Curt Chelin

17547

So you need to use the **library**!

Hang on! Help is on the way!

If you have a hard time

- understanding how the library works,
- talking with the librarian, or
- finding books and other materials in the library...

...you are not alone.

Just in case you're wondering...

...why don't we start at the beginning?

What is a Library?

A library is a place where books, magazines, and other resource materials are stored. These materials are not for sale but can be borrowed or used free of charge.

The major purpose of the library is to provide resources that will make it easy for you to
- find information you may want or need, and
- find books for your reading enjoyment.

The library is a quiet, friendly place where you can go to read, think, and study. It is also a special place that can help you in many ways. Here are just a few examples:

- The library can save you time and effort.

- The library can save you money.

- The library can help you with your schoolwork.

- The library can entertain you.

The Librarians

Librarians are people who work in the library. They have had special training and are experts in the field of library science. You will find that librarians can be a great resource and are more than willing to help you locate material.

When you are working with your librarians, it will help to keep these things in mind:

- Let them get to know you. It is easier for them to help you when they know a little about you.
- When asking questions, be clear and precise.
- Be polite and patient. There are many people who need the librarian's help.
- If you need a lot of help, call and make an appointment to meet with one of the librarians.
- Show your appreciation for the time and effort they give you.

The Library Card

You are welcome to use any of the materials in the library. If you wish to take some of the materials with you, you will need a library card. Most public libraries issue cards free of charge. Owning a library card is a privilege and a responsibility.

- You are responsible for making sure your card is not lost or stolen.
- You are responsible for any books or materials that are checked out on your card.
- You are responsible for any fines charged against your card.

Library Rules

Every library has its own rules. Here are some rules you will be expected to follow in every library:

- Be quiet.
- Handle the materials with care.
- Never write in the books.
- Return books on time.
- Pay fines promptly.
- Do *not* reshelve books.

The library can be a great resource that you can use throughout your life. First, you need to learn *how* to use it. The key to using the library is understanding how it is organized. Here is a general introduction to how the library system works.

The Card Catalog

Most libraries have thousands of books in their collection. With so many books, it is necessary for each library to keep an index of what books it has and where the books are located. This index is called the card catalog. If you are going to use the library, you must learn how to use the card catalog.

The card catalog is usually located in a central area in the library. It is made up of long, narrow drawers that are labeled and arranged in alphabetical order.

Inside the drawers of the card catalog are thousands of 3 by 5 cards. These cards contain valuable information about every book in the library. The cards are arranged in alphabetical order from A to Z and include special guide cards. These guide cards help you find the books you need quickly and easily.

Using the Card Catalog

There are three ways to locate a book in the card catalog. You can look up
- the title of the book,
- the author's name, or
- the subject heading.

In some libraries, all of this information is included in one card catalog. Other libraries divide this information into two separate catalogs, one according to author-title, and one by subject heading.

The method you use to locate a book depends on the information you already have about the book.

- If you know the title, look for the title card.
- If you don't know the title, but know the author's name, look for the author card.
- If you know only what the book is about, or if you have a subject you want to investigate, look for the subject card.

Title Cards

Every book in the library has a title card in the card catalog. On this card, the title of the book is the first line you see at the top of the card.

The title card is filed in alphabetical order according to the words in the title.

Author Cards

Every book in the library also has an author card in the card catalog. On this card, the name of the person who wrote the book is the first line you see at the top of the card.

The author card is filed in alphabetical order according to the author's last name.

Subject Card

Every nonfiction and some fiction books have at least one subject card in the card catalog. On this card, the subject area covered in the book is the first line you see at the top of the card.

The subject card is filed in alphabetical order according to the words in the subject heading.

As you look up cards in the card catalog, keep these things in mind:

- If a title starts with the word "A," "An," or "The," the card will be filed according to the next word in the title.
- If the title starts with an abbreviation or a number, the card is filed as if the words are spelled out. For example, U.S. would be filed as United States, and 100 as one hundred.

Cross Reference Cards

As you look up cards in the card catalog, you may come across a cross reference card. There are two types of these cards:

"See" Card. If you do not find any material under the subject heading you are using, you may find a "See" card. This card refers you to another subject heading.

"See Also" Card. This card offers you some extra help. It can give you ideas for other subject areas to look up that are related to your topic.

Reading the Catalog Card

The catalog card contains a lot of valuable information other than the title, author, and subject heading. It has information that can help you decide which books you want before you actually see the books. Here is some of the information you can discover from the catalog card:

- *Co-authors*—gives you the names of authors of the book.
- *Illustrations*—tells you if there are any illustrations, and what kind.
- *Illustrator*—tells you who drew the illustrations.
- *Location and name of publisher*—tells you who the publisher is and where the book was published in case you want to purchase the book from the publisher.
- *Copyright date*—tells you if the material is recent enough to have accurate and current information.
- *Number of pages*—helps you determine how thoroughly the topic is covered.
- *Summary*—tells you what information is covered in the book.
- *Call number*—tells you where to find the book in the library if you want it.
- *Bibliography*—gives you a list of other sources.

SUBJECT HEADING
GARDENING
AUTHOR
TITLE
CO-AUTHOR
ILLUSTRATOR
599.02 M
Moss, Pete
Eating Your Garden, by Pete Moss & Clay Potts; illustrated by Ida Hoe.
New York, Green Publishing House, c 1983.
101 p. : ill.
How to plant a vegetable garden.
Bibliography: p95-97
CALL NUMBER
NUMBER OF PAGES
LOCATION AND NAME OF PUBLISHER
COPYRIGHT DATE
SUMMARY
HAS ILLUSTRATIONS
HAS BIBLIOGRAPHY
SO THAT'S WHAT ALL THAT STUFF MEANS!

Before you leave the card catalog to find the books you want to use, you need to do one more thing. Write down all the important information for each book, so you won't have to look up the books in the card catalog again. Be sure to include these things:
- the full title,
- the author's name, and
- the call number if you are looking up a nonfiction book.

Finding the Books on the Shelves

Once you have decided which books you want, you will need to find out where the books are located. This process is different for fiction books and nonfiction books.

Fiction is something that is *not* true. Fiction books are usually located in a separate section of the library. They are arranged alphabetically according to the author's last name. Here's how to locate a fiction book:
- Go to the fiction section of the library.
- Find the shelf by looking for the author's name.
- Find the book by looking for the title.

Nonfiction is something that *is* true. Nonfiction books are usually classified according to a numbering system. Every book is assigned a call number which appears on the book's catalog card and on the spine of the book. Here's how to locate a nonfiction book:
- Find the book listed in the card catalog.
- Carefully copy down the book's call number, author, and title.
- Find the number among the nonfiction shelves.
- Find the book you want in that number area by looking for the author and title.

Books are not the only resources you will find listed in the card catalog. Many libraries have films, filmstrips, records, and tapes listed in the card catalog as well. You never know what you'll find.

To save space, some libraries are putting their card catalog on microfiche or on a computer. If you know how to use the card catalog, learning to use the microfiche or computer catalog will be easy. If your library has a microfiche or computer catalog, ask your librarian to show you how to use it.

REFERENCE BOOKS

There is a section in your library that is set aside for reference books. These books are designed to give you specific information about a subject. Each reference book gives you a different kind of information. Most reference books cannot be checked out, but you can photocopy any important information that you need to take with you.

How you choose a reference book depends on the kind of information you need. Here are some of the major reference books and the different kinds of information they provide:

The Encyclopedia

This is a series of books that provides an overview of information about most major subject areas. The encyclopedia is a good place to look for general information about any topic.

The Dictionary

There are many types of dictionaries in the reference section. A *word dictionary* provides information about words. It tells you how to spell a word, how to pronounce a word, and what the word means. A *biographical dictionary* gives you important facts about famous people.

The Atlas and Gazetteers

These books provide information about geography. The atlas is a collection of maps that is designed to give you information about places on the earth. The gazetteer is a dictionary of geography that provides facts about places on the earth.

Almanacs and Other Yearbooks

These books provide current facts about many subjects. The almanac is a yearbook of general facts about a wide range of subjects. There are also yearbooks that specialize in facts about one certain subject.

It is a good idea to browse through the reference section of your library to see what reference books are available. You might also want to ask your librarian to show you how to use them. This will prepare you for those times when you will need this type of information.

MAGAZINES, NEWSPAPERS, AND PAMPHLETS

Sometimes, you will need information that is not available in books. This information can be found in several other library sources, such as magazines, newspapers, and pamphlets. These sources, however, are not listed in the card catalog. Each of these sources has its own special index.

Magazines

The library has several indexes that list magazine articles. There is one index that lists the articles printed in over 170 popular magazines. This index is called *The Reader's Guide to Periodical Literature*. *The Reader's Guide* is published two times a month. This makes it possible to look up information that is very current.

The Reader's Guide is much like the card catalog in book form. It helps you find articles on a subject you may need or want to investigate. The articles are listed alphabetically by author and subject. An entry might look like this:

Note: if the abbreviations seem confusing at first, there is a key that explains them in the front of *The Reader's Guide.*

When you find several articles that look interesting:
1. Write down for each one
   - name of the magazine,
   - title of the article,
   - author's name,
   - volume number,
   - date of issue, and
   - page numbers.
2. Check to see if the magazines you want are available at your library. Your library will have a list of magazines it subscribes to.
3. Go to the magazine area and look for the issues you need. If you can't find them, ask your librarian for help.

Newspapers

The newspaper is one of the best sources of information for current events. Many libraries keep their local newspapers on file and store back issues on microfilm. Many libraries also have large city newspapers such as *The New York Times*. These newspapers contain important national and world news.

The Vertical File

Your library has pamphlets and other miscellaneous materials that are hard to store. These materials are kept in a filing cabinet called the vertical file. The materials are arranged by subject matter and usually include a wide variety of information.

Now you have an overview of the many resources your library has to offer. To learn even more about your library, set aside an afternoon and ask your librarian for a tour of your library. It will make the information in this book more meaningful to you, and it could be the beginning of an important friendship.

WARNING!

If you learn the things in this book...

ALL RIGHT!

...you will have a world of knowledge at your finger tips.

THE END

About the Author
Marilyn Berry has a master's degree in education with a specialization in reading. She is on staff as a producer and creator of supplementary materials at the Institute of Living Skills. Marilyn is a published author of books and composer of music for children. She is the mother of two sons, John and Brent.